Praise for Rafael Campo

"Rafael Campo is one of the most gifted and accomplished younger poets writing in English. More than that, he is a writer engaged in several of the pivotal struggles and issues of our era, and what he has to say about them is 'news that stays news.'"—Marilyn Hacker

"Campo's background and concerns—he writes out of his identity and experience as a gay Cuban American physician—make for a rich field of investigations, and his best work is both passionate and formally accomplished. *What the Body Told* dives into the difficult, necessary territory of physical love, desire, contagion, illness; such poems are essential to our moment. We need them."—Mark Doty

"Campo is one of the most attractive, interesting and—I can think of no better word—*valuable* poets of his generation. The news he has to tell is the news we need, and his talent, happily, is equal to his message."—Richard Howard

"[A] virtuoso display. . . . Campo is a master of image. . . . His poems are revealing and courageous."—Jay A. Liveson, *Journal of the American Medical Association*

"Campo writes mordant lyrics of dark love that displace trite expectations of what sonnets or *canciones* should accomplish. His work is devoid of cheap romanticizing."—Jerry W. Ward Jr., *Washington Post Book World*

"Campo's heartfelt prose is the real thing. He lays himself bare and in the process creates art."—*Library Journal*

"I know of no poet writing today with more courage and compassion than Rafael Campo. Like the practicing physician that he is, Campo writes poems that heal artfully—or honestly face the impossibility of healing. Here we find sonnets for the damned, songs for the dying, the insistence on empathy for a prostitute with AIDS on a Boston street corner. There is the unforgiving squint of a mother rejecting her gay son. Yet there is a soaring lyricism in these poems, epiphany and redemption, a celebration of bloodstained, stubborn life as it bursts forth. The poems of Rafael Campo inspire that sharp breath of recognition. He has all my gratitude and admiration."
—Martín Espada, author of *Imagine the Angels of Bread*

"Extraordinary meditations on illness and the healing power of words."—*Lambda Literary Foundation*

"Rafael Campo is perhaps our most distinguished physician-poet since William Carlos Williams. . . . [His] sense of a common humanity is hard-won against the ugliness, misery, and cruelty that he must confront in his practice."—David Bergman, *The Gay and Lesbian Review*

Landscape with Human Figure

Rafael Campo

LANDSCAPE WITH HUMAN FIGURE

Duke University Press Durham and London 2002

Designed by C. H. Westmoreland

Typeset in Carter & Cohn Galliard by

Tseng Information Systems, Inc.

Library of Congress

Cataloging-in-Publication Data

Campo, Rafael.

Landscape with human figure / Rafael Campo.

p. cm.

ISBN 0-8223-2875-5 (acid-free paper) —

ISBN 0-8223-2890-9 (pbk. : acid-free paper)

1. Cuban Americans—Poetry. 2. Medicine—

Poetry. 3. Gay men—Poetry. I. Title.

PS3553.A4883 L36 2002

811'.54—dc21   2001047057

The promotion, marketing, and distribution
of this book are supported by a generous grant
from the Gill Foundation.

for my parents, who taught me to love

for Jorge, who brought me to life

Dominion strong is the body's; dominion stronger is the mind's.

—Walt Whitman, *Democratic Vistas*

And my "medicine" was the thing which gained me entrance to these secret gardens of the self.

—William Carlos Williams, *Of Medicine and Poetry*

Contents

Acknowledgments

I am grateful to the editors of the following periodicals in which some of these poems have appeared, sometimes in slightly different forms: the *Antioch Review,* the *Bark,* the *Bellevue Literary Review, Black Book, Callaloo, Connect,* the *Cortland Review, CROWD, Eyeball,* the *Gay and Lesbian Review,* the *Isle Review* (formerly *Isle*), *Nerve,* the *New England Review,* the *New Republic, Pleiades, Ploughshares, Provincetown Arts, River Styx, Slate,* the *Threepenny Review, TriQuarterly,* the *Western Humanities Review,* and *Yemassee.*

"The Couple" first appeared in *Doctors Afield* (Yale University Press, 1999).

LANDSCAPE WITH HUMAN FIGURE

On New Year's Day

If hopefulness resides in what we can
resolve to change, then let us give up sweets,
nail-biting, cigarettes, the habits of
our weak humanity—we *can* succeed

if only we try hard enough, resist
potato chips and shed ten pounds, return
whatever book we have that's overdue,
forgive inequities and do what's just—

because today is anything, it is
our natural color, it is when we
begin to save, it is the better spouse
we'll be, it is beginning to be free.

Nightfall in Asturias

Like eyebrows raised with weary resignation,
the arches of the Roman bridges here
bear witness to the endless passage not
of pilgrims now, but tourists. Equal in
the terrible iniquities of sin
if not in abnegation of the self,
we photograph the Lord's profane creation:
the darkly ugly family of boar
that wallows on the river's edge, a plot
plowed neatly into rows of rocky earth

that clings against a mountain's flank, a bus
with "Bimbo" blazoned on its side (a brand
of cake in Spain that makes some giggle — men,
of course, who are Americans like us).
The curving roads we travel parallel
the northern route the faithful took to find
the shrine where James the Greater's lost remains
were finally discovered, centuries
ago. The sun sets slow as a saint bleeds,
eternal reds; fake Rolexes for sale,

spread out like treasures from a foreign land,
attract a couple to a gypsy's table.
I watch you as you puzzle over maps,
perplexed myself by what, if anything,
it is that joins us. Not the sin, because
we're all guilty of the abominable;
not lack of fear, because I know the loss
of you would be much more than I could stand.
I grasp it when the gypsies start to sing
of night as sanctuary, love as hope.

Quatrains for a Shrinking World

I. *El Oriental de Cuba, "La Esquina del Sabor"*

Victorians surrounding it, the place
is just a storefront restaurant that seats
about a dozen people; strange, to taste
roast pork that's drenched in *mojo,* yuca *frites,*

and milkshakes of *mamey* this far up North.
Outside, if they were still alive, I might
expect my grandparents to pass, the force
of their unending exile not quite

enough to stop them—only slow them down.
Abuela, stooped by bags of groceries,
her makeup's compensation overdone;
and Granpa, brittle as his misery,

his guayabera barely filled by bones.
I wonder whether she'd prepare *congrí*
for him, upon their safe arrival home.
If only they could get there, finally.

II. Writer in Exile

I've wished that I were born a Soviet,
so that my presence in America
would cause as greatly dignified regret
as leads to literary coup d'états—

but I am merely Cuban, dark and small
as any from a hundred nations which
exist for others' domination. All
I say is colonized, if not by rich

"protectors," then by communists who redden
on Varadero Beach; my poetry,
if plagued by form, otherwise does not threaten
(conveniently) the New-World-Orderly

procession of the vanquished. Hear my voice,
my queerly Spanish intonation, hear
the perfect sound of banishment. Rejoice!
I'm nothing yet, although tomorrow's near.

III. Take-Out Night with Friends:

A Meditation on "Multiculturalism"

Half French-Canadian, half African-
American, my friend is marrying
an Irish-Chinese man; the Indian
and German-Scottish couple always bring

their daughter to our get-togethers, where
my partner and I host, conventional
first-time homeowners—gay, or even queer
(and yes, Latino too), we seem of all

our group the most bourgeois. We gaze at her,
the tiny, lovely Nina Clair, her skin
a color neither cinnamon nor pure
white ivory, but somewhere in between;

she smiles at her "uncles," six months old
still young enough to trust, to love without
"diversity." Perhaps she sees the world
in us. Or else, she's slowly learning doubt.

IV. The Modern Cartographer's Lament

My globe confuses me with distances.
An island only ninety miles lee
fades infinitely far, while Budapest
(at least the part that's Little Hungary)

thrives only blocks from where I shop street stands.
If only hatred didn't travel just
as paradoxically: the African-
American whose tortured death defaced

the Texas hills, the NATO bombs unloosed
upon the Balkans. Here, right here, I see
each horror, all as near as neighborhood—
as if these continents were joined, these seas

unfilled by tears none ever had to cry.
I plot out borders nature never made,
the shapes of nations random to my eye
whose peoples wander, equal in their need.

V. Never Home

I'm never home, no matter where I go.
My loneliness is everywhere: in sand
I see the ruined castles I once owned;
the breeze forgets me, though it comes again.

I'm never home, despite the calls of birds
I recognize in my back yard: they lie
about the beautiful and the absurd.
They're calming, but to others' heartless cries.

I'm never home, though if I were I guess
I wouldn't know the customs of my doomed,
disbanded race: proper forms of address,
rules governing small talk in living rooms,

directions to the dimming corridor
of houselights that I'll never find. I close
my eyes, the evening's dark my paramour;
I'm all our pain, consoled in his embrace.

VI. America, The Beautiful

Saluting it, I half-forgot I was
a fag, a spic, a goddamn immigrant—
it was *so beautiful, for spacious skies*
I thought that even I was maybe meant

to be a part of it, that melting pot
(that later, in the seventh grade, was salad)—
I thought that maybe all the shit I got
would make me sing it better, not a ballad,

an anthem for the strongest land on earth.
I couldn't help it though, the way my voice
would rise a bit too high beyond my worth,
my classmates snickering from verse to verse,

my teacher looking stonily away.
America, America I shed
no tears beneath your drooping flag that day;
I sang more loudly, as Cubans do, instead.

VII. Poem.com

Parisian laces, Pakistani rugs,
wrought iron from Australia; Russian guns,
South African folk art, Honduran rums . . .
The Internet makes owning worlds of fun:

From Boston, I can have it all! I trade
my stocks on-line; the fortune I amass
through virtual verisimilitude
will fuel my buying power while it lasts,

this universe of what is possible
for any sybarite to have. Today,
postmodernly I ventured to Brazil
and browsed the Amazon for butterflies

so rare they ought to be extinct by now;
I paid the Indians with Coke and beads
for specimens bright as my computer's glow.
I'll press them in the books I never read.

VIII. "Aunt Paula's Here, Time to Say Good Bye. . ."

They left the TV on for us. The screen
would fill with places that they visited:
Morocco, Mexico, the Philippines.
They left us, sadly maybe, tucked in beds

in which we dreamed the world was safe for them,
for us, the crickets' voices small enough
to seem familiar, wind outside the hymn
of many nations joined in peace. They loved

to travel then; they left us, memories
they half-remember now, their boys asleep
behind a darkened window, the TV's
ghosts dancing all around us, quietly—

I like to think of them, their suitcase heavy,
the night grown thick, still turning in the black
toward home, in leaving us knowing every
last journey, however far, ends in coming back.

The Blackouts

In Cuba, when the power dies at night,
They point the headlights of their rumbling cars—
Old Cadillacs and Chevys, relics of
A brighter time—to flood their crumbling rooms
With light. They're going nowhere, yet they face
The engines of an industry that if
It wanted to, might crush them. On their backs,
They take a swig of rum; they're comforted,
Perhaps, by someone else's touch, the taste
Of salt that's in the breeze with the exhaust.
Imagine how gigantic are their shadows,
Projected on the dingy walls—how far
The world must seem, that spites the open windows—
Imagine that they're climbing in, at last,
Their roaring ride to freedom past the stars,
Across the seas, interminable, like ours.

Ghazal in a Time of War

for Agha Shahid Ali

What spoke to me, that wasn't words at all
but like a language, understood by all:

Ducks arrowing their way across the small,
dark pond I passed, graceful emblem of all

I like to think is Spring, their pace a crawl.
My own unhurried progress—after all,

awaiting me was just the usual,
the ill who are my daily "chores"—was all

that I could muster, kids on bicycles
zig-zagging by, a Russian couple all

wrapped up in smoky conversation, tall
oaks pointing out the white sun . . . Was it all

just my imagination? I recall
those sounds of the world, the joy of it all,

the toddler whose face was a miracle
as she chased her red ball. Please, save it all,

I think I prayed, above the distant bombs' shrill
descent; please, please, remember that we're all

one people, one body, one chance not to kill.
A stray gull cried, but that was not all:

I saw where I was going, past the arsenal
and past the land mine, to the land of all,

past the archangel and the syllable,
toward our human heart, to the love of all.

Outside Fayetteville

I

Come north to harvest strawberries and corn,
I wonder what this family of four
disheveled Mexicans must think of us:
they buy a few things at a corner store
outside of which are parked two pick-ups, one
displaying Dixie's "Stars and Bars" inside
the cab's rear window. Never looking up,
the little girl (perhaps in school) has learned
already something that it says about
her place; her father, still an immigrant,
regards it with a curiosity,
a kind of hopeful sympathy, that seems
to ask *What country have you fled, and why?*

II

A black man walks along the road beneath
a billboard advertising "Southern Pride!"
He's shirtless in the blazing midday heat,
and pauses in the shade afforded by
the giant cut-out, rippling emblem. Sweat
is dripping off him like a baptism,
the ritual absolving us of what
we never should forget. The sky glares white
above the bold-faced "New Economy,"
the promise of another better day
when all, God willing, shall be judged not by
the color of their skin, but by their "CLOUT."
The black man, slowly moving onward, gleams.

What I Would Give

What I would like to give them for a change
is not the usual prescription with
its hubris of the power to restore,
to cure; what I would like to give them, ill
from not enough of laying in the sun
not caring what the onlookers might think
while feeding some banana to their dogs—
what I would like to offer them is this,
not reassurance that their lungs sound fine,
or that the mole they've noticed change is not
a melanoma, but instead of fear
transfigured by some doctorly advice
I'd like to give them my astonishment
at sudden rainfall like the whole world weeping,
and how ridiculously gently it
slicked down my hair; I'd like to give them that,
the joy I felt while staring in your eyes
as you learned epidemiology
(the science of disease in populations),
the night around our bed like timelessness,
like comfort, like what I would give to them.

For My Brother's Wedding

in honor of Mark and Gabriela

My brother is the restless type, renowned
for his extreme adventures. He has climbed

a Himalayan peak, swum naked in
a bioluminescent bay at dawn,

and even had a motorcycle crush
his ankle in some unmapped part of Greece.

My brother did these things when he was young
despite the limitations of his lungs,

beset (by asthma and by cigarettes)
with coughing I was worried I might get—

(I thought tuberculosis suited me,
the quailing poet earning his M.D.)

though his exposures far exceeded mine,
which then to textbooks only were confined.

I had this vision of him conquering
the globe I'd read about in books, with long

black hair, sun-burnished skin, and muscled arms
we studied in the photos from afar

that made him seem a cross between a bear
and some new Indian B-movie star.

I'd think of him some nights, the library
at midnight like an empty, flood-lit sea:

my brother, two vast continents away,
a cigarette between his lips, a day

of trekking burning in his legs, alone
but not afraid, not here but never gone,

the kind of distance that sparked memory.
I would remember playing underneath

the trees at Nonna's house, the ghostly hollow
through which the blinking fireflies we'd follow

a place we could imagine anything—
like mountain-climbing, even marrying

the perfect girls that he'd invent. Today
my brother realizes what we'd say

years later, having found that woman; I
look back on all his travels, modified

in me through our adulthood into pride,
and mark the stunning beauty of his bride

(herself more rare than all of this world's wonders,
some Venus from a temple never plundered),

and somehow still I want to give advice
that older-brother's habit in my voice

of thinking that I'd always known—as if
he'd not—our greatest journey is in love.

Landscape with Human Figure

Arguably, it is less beautiful
because of you. A sweeping vista, trees
discernable along a river's bank
where one imagines how a darkening
of colors in the quiet shade must feel—
not cool so much as safe, not wet but dank—
as if the artist somehow painted song
a bird the viewer doesn't really see

lets wane. Of course, without you there would be
no purpose for this act of definition.
The world would be content to stay like this,
serenely unobserved, a living space
whose margins physically extend beyond
the tricks of what is called deceptively
"perspective" or "technique." You stand
unmoving like the landscape, your sole mission

to register the grandeur, witness joy,
remain as silent as the wind that shaped
the clouds above you. Less than beautiful,
I recognize myself in you; the sky
is very blue, so blue I want to fall
from it to earth, through the enormity
of yearning and of disbelief—a hope
that, if I ever reach you, rescues me.

SPEAK TO ME

In Praise of Experience

My memories lack eloquence, too fresh
to resonate with anything I see
today, as to the post office I slosh
through February's snow-then-rain. Two trees,
whose leafless branches looked like skeletons
in x-rays in my windows' viewboxes,
remind me of disease, but yet to come;
describing new things that their baby does
or prospects for their next great jobs, my friends
seem innocently far from tragedy.
Beneath a rusting, tilted scaffold stand
a dozen or so people, wet like me.
They're looking up, regarding quietly
a complex rescue operation: men
in yellow hardhats have discovered three
small kittens hidden in a makeshift den
where next another steel beam's to go.
The high-pitched mewing sounds like violins.
Their protests recollect how long ago—
exactly what? My youth was full of sins
and awful yearnings that, through the fine mist
of present weather and such little time,
seem easily domesticated myths.
i'm all too readily explained, defined
by facile similes that poetry
even cannot dignify. In years from now,
much wiser, skeptical, I want to be
a witness once again, my wrinkled brow
less bothered by the chilling wind; my chores
will offer nothing in the way of newness,
as I'll have done them countless times before.
And when I pause, I want what's first a nuisance
to prompt a moment of deep thought, I want
to understand the meaning of this scene—
this banal circumstance, magnificent—
as I remember I was younger once.

October Afternoon, 1986

Leaves burning somewhere, traces of blue smoke
a sweet autumnal aphrodisiac—
we struggled over the equations, cloaked
in life's organic secrecies. Your back,

as you leaned over glucose forming bonds
with oxygen, was broad and strong; your leg
was pressing into mine, while all around
the college seemed too temporal to beg

the question any longer. Tenting out
my jeans, my surging, rock-hard cock propelled
me to your dorm. You put your mouth to it,
the rising breeze still tinged with fire's smell;

my hands began to strip you of your sweats,
and when I saw the curve of your erection,
thick, heavy with desire, what love begets
became what we were. Natural selection,

imaginary numbers, clouds of bright
electrons, calculus; when we were spent,
a weightless cinder drifted through the dimming light
to settle on my chest. Into flames, the day went.

Oysters

Your concentration while you're shucking them
Is fierce: they fight against your prying blade,
As if intent to guard some plumbless gem
Of truth. I squeeze some fruit for lemonade;
The yellow rinds become a fragrant pile.
More scraping from the deck, a stifled curse—
You bring me one, the frilly muscle pale,
Defeated, silent in its briny juice
Like sweat expended in the effort to
Remain inviolate. I slurp it down,
One dose of aphrodisiac, and you
Return to your grim work, all Provincetown
Draped out below you, edge of the known world.
I see what is left: bone-white, hollow-shelled.

Your Black Eyes

All I could think of was the time we first
discovered what two men could do: your fist

around my rigid cock, yours in my mouth.
You talked about the reasons why, about

the grey unhappiness of us, routines,
monotonous discussions, stupid scenes

(the restaurant, the dry cleaner's). Outside,
some shirtless Puerto Rican kids made night

pulse dangerous again, like when we kissed
in that dark alleyway, your cold hand pressed

inside my jeans. You talked about how hard
it was for you, and how I never heard

what you were saying all these years; the sound
of distant barking dogs—complaining—seemed

if not forthright, at least forgivable.
God, how I wanted to fuck you until

the red light of dawn injured us as one,
until inside of you I'd almost come—

our love familiar as our furniture,
as urgent as your black eyes' needful stare—

but you were leaving me that night, and sex
is always only what the other wrecks.

Playing "Fidel and Perón"

When you are kissing me, the whole world sighs.
Havana joins with Buenos Aires in
our rapturous embrace, all night
a kind of heated argument about
our excesses, about lost empire. Try
to understand how being loved by you
is something I once only fantasized,
the club of my hard-on pressed to your thigh
as two men danced a tango like they used
to do; resist the urge to comprehend

how passionate ideas cause us harm.
When you are kissing me, the world is tears
of mourning, of forgiveness. In your arms,
it's something more like need than brotherhood
that makes me whisper Spanish poetry
against your ear, and what we want seems both
not revolutionary and unfeared.
I play some salsa as I run our bath,
a tiny, candlelit, demilitarized sea
in which two strongmen squander all they had.

On Valentine's Day

We're not a married couple, though today
We let ourselves pretend we are. We walk
Together holding hands outside, afraid
Of nothing. Lost in recipes, I cook
A dinner too outlandish, while you plot
To buy me something I can't really use.
You call me silly nicknames ("Tater Tot"
Is one that makes me cringe); I look at you
A little wistfully, believing love is real,
And do things equally ridiculous,
Like sit in places you've just left to feel
Your warmth seep into me. The two of us,
Together all these years, forget we are
Two men who'll never marry, still just queers.

Last Hours in Florence

I

North Africans sell tiny replicas
Of famous statues to the tourists swarmed
Inside the huge piazza; punked-out kids,
Tomorrow's Michelangelos, seem armed
For battle by their body piercings. WHY
KILLED KOSOVO is punctuated by
A blood-red skull whose art I can't deny—
Writ timelessly on marble just beside
The spot where centuries ago were burned
Great books and music, paintings deemed profane.
A stylish older woman walks behind
Her equally well-groomed Dalmatian, trained,
It's clear, to stay nearby without a leash.
I study them, and think this whole café
Is democratic in its double wish
For beauty and for its control. The day
Is near its end, here in the part of the world
Where all is remembered, and nothing dread—
The church bells sound, by God's and human will—
I understand why they must ring again.
In Santa Barbara, the place we might
Be from someday, the same hot sun lays bare
A truth more personal, yet like in weight.
We disagree about the need for fear.

II

A car alarm goes off—the room's slight view
Includes a parking lot, above which rise
The distant hills and terra-cotta roofs
That could console some hapless lover whose
Abandonment is unforgivable.
In everything, it seems, I am aware
Of absences, the shrieking loss of all
I thought I understood about this world.
Beneath the beauty, there's an awful void,
As if what *David* tries to occupy
(That spectacle of largeness but a boy)
Could ever be assuaged. About to cry
But stifling his tears, a teenager
Runs out to turn the wailing off—he's chased
By someone twice his age who yells a slur
That even in Italian I can place.
Unwillingly, I try to catch his eye,
As if in anonymity I could
Restore an even deeper peace. The sky
Begins to offer us its ransom gold.
Who broke his heart, I want to know, *who killed*
His innocent belief in love? We're all
Conspirators, bereft of something we once felt
But that we're never able to recall.

III

Enough of sightseeing, enough of wine—
My appetites seem permanently dulled.
I'm tired of the dirt and the divine.
The endless mopeds once seemed comical,
A cross between mosquitos and Beijing
That now just sputter and annoy; though God's
Imprisoned back behind the scaffolding,
I'm sure He disapproves of all things plaid,
Especially bermuda shorts. Outside
Its walls, like ants on something very sweet,
The tourists snap their photographs beside
The patient pink-and-green cathedral. Weeks
Ago, I felt a similar surprise,
I guess, on looking up from my creased map
To the distant century that met my eyes.
We sat right down, your hand warm in my lap,
Oblivious to those whose way we blocked.
We sat there, silently, a bit afraid
Of all we hadn't learned to talk
About: magnificence, at once betrayed
Yet heightened by our flawed humanity.
On leaving Florence, what I want to say
Is that I'm sorry if it wasn't me
Who found forgiveness when he lost his way.

IV

It rained all day when we arrived; the clouds
Reminded me of Santa Barbara,
Dramatic, climbing up the mountainsides
To make mysterious their peaks. A ray
Of sun for just a moment lit a house
In golds and oranges before it went—
A gilded domesticity (like ours?)
Too suddenly extinguished. Reticent,
The raindrops fell like tears that can't be held
Inside for shame; you told me that tomorrow
It would be beautiful again, your hold
On me quite confident before the window,
Mirrored upon the bleary view. This trip
Was something that you'd always promised me:
Our happiness deferred, I'd learned to stop
Expecting luxuries like Italy,
Preferring the ornate palazzo of
My loneliness, in which on every wall
Were hung the tributes of a kind of love:
Grand portraiture, beneath which I seemed small.
The train to Genoa departed late,
And so we're here, ungrateful for the gift
Of what grey industry must make—the freight
Of voyages—as the leaden clouds lift.

Speak to Me

Because the dictionary won't,
Because the novel's not around,
I ask that you please speak to me.

Internet, comic books; billboards' rant.
Words are everywhere, without sound.
I ask that someone speak to me.

Even TV and the movies can't.
I want your language to astound.
You must, you have to speak to me,

To touch me with your throat's descant,
To comfort, make me understand.
I'm begging you to speak with me—

Your voice that is intelligent,
Your intonation that resounds,
You'll talk and talk all night with me,

Above the howls, the moon's ascent,
Above the neighbors' bump and grind,
You'll tell it true, and just for me—

Until the morning's argument
And newspapers that never end
God damn you, speak again, it's me

But unsaid words will have you then,
When even poets won't defend
Such silences as speak to me.

Poem for My Familiar

She's sniffing out the garden's rancid truths,
beneath the garbage cans, along the roots

arthritically attaching oaks to earth—
she means to do her business, back and forth

not nervously as much as in pursuit
of some unnamed perfection. Reddish coat

and barrel chest, the sleek embodiment
of what? Not loyalty so much as want,

not pleasure but the wish to please. Her piss
pools darkly; sudden wind makes the oaks hiss.

She trots off, proud of her obedience
(our countless warnings adding up to sense)

and in her I catch something of myself,
that eagerness with which I sought relief

pretending there was nothing wrong with us.
You call to me, your voice too serious

for scolding dawdlers on a summer day,
and Ruby charges by. I think I'll stay

behind, but soon think better of it. Still,
although I love you, it's unbearable

to watch you growing distant. Ruby yelps,
but somehow all her playfulness won't help:

like her, I want to beg forgiveness for
my mute mistakes, my urgent need for more.

After Losing Him

The sky is reddening. The leaves come down,
one here, one there, as if deliberate
in their intent to cover up the lawn.
Embarrassed by its excesses, the late

autumnal afternoon would like to fade
to something closer to a mournful black.
The sky is reddening, guilt turned to blood.
I sit in silence here, as if I could un-break

the heart that welcomes death. What I would give
to understand it all as utterly—
to give you up unwillingly, to love
despite the wanton sky that shushes me

with long, sweet fingers. Then, with darkest night
descending, first stars like bits of peace,
stiff leaves sinking to the cold lawn, how light
at last extinguishes. None but us sees.

AFRAID OF THE DARK

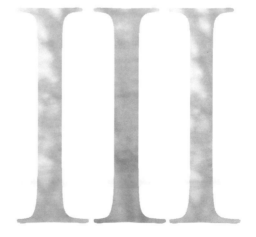

Afraid of the Dark

The figure entered silently. The clock
ticked urgently, impossibly too loud,
a warning in the humid, hungry black.
Mosquito netting swathed me, paralyzed—
a plaintive heartbeat through a fog of fear.
The figure loomed, and imperceptibly
examined items on my desk—my clear
white plastic protractor that slightly gleamed
like half the moon, my figurine of Luke
whose blond hair shimmered when I made him kill
Darth Vader, then my spiral notebook blank
and white suspended in the dark. Stock-still
I watched the figure, waiting for the knife
to be displayed, with which he'd end my life—

a curved machete like the gardener's,
as if on cue, hooked back the netting like
an awful talon. Shrinking from his stare,
I forced my eyes shut—all I saw was black,
his face, his torn T-shirt, his dungarees—
the images of evil I had always known
made real. The figure shifted when I screamed,
and it was seconds later, when light shone
from up above—my father flicked it on—
that I could glimpse his startled, pale face,
before he jettisoned the knife and ran.
I don't know why I lied about his race,
describing him to the police. I guess
I wanted them to capture something else.

This family in the commercial for
McDonald's couldn't possibly be us.
It's not just that they're black, caricatures
made up by ad execs to paraphrase
some liberal pretense of tolerance
that some of us recite inside ourselves—
I am not racist when I buy cream rinse—
it is their eagerness to please us, salve
the injury of what we are afraid
is true. The television, just this once,
imparts some wisdom as we watch them fed
as much by the American past tense
(it never happened here) as by Big Macs
and fragile, golden fries that we know blacks

just love. They're us, but then they're not because
I can't know what it means to be ignored
while customers whose skin is white are served
attentively—to have my very words
rewritten for a script that has to sell.
The desperation of a Happy Meal
that can't convince the world that we are full,
that we are equal, joined in what we feel—
in perfect English, how the little girl
is forced to be only her prettiness,
her shiny hair controlled in braids that swirl
into the vortex of bright white that says
although she's starved, she's lucky to be here
and she must never, ever ask for more.

The dream of being black I had arose
from what might seem a cave of helplessness—
arriving here, this land of surplus and repose,
I was surprised to find my genes a mess!
A deep anxiety about what was
"my share" had stricken at the heart of me.
I danced with Michael Jackson; through the gauze,
I knew he saw that I'd had surgery
to make my features look more African.
The sweat dripped down my face and stung
my slowly-healing scars, and that was when
the blaring disco started darkening.
The rich white kids from nearby suburbs ran,
their diamond jewelry glinting in the acrid rain

of strobe and flame that fell upon the crowd.
Though there was nothing I could do, I felt
perversely powerful as while they cried
the blackness crawled across my skin. My guilt
half-seemed resolved; my people's owning slaves,
my reflex racist finger-pointing, all
of it destroyed in the inferno's blaze.
Alone, I searched amid the spectacle
of ruin left behind when it was done,
but Michael and the rest had disappeared.
From somewhere came the eerie drone
of what I'd call a love song born of fear.
Last chance for romance, the voice declaimed.
In all my blackness, beauty mixed with pain.

We gaze at them, above us at a kind
of distance I imagine "homeland" is.
Their names are strange to me as Spanish. Lined
with worry, in his face are darknesses
the lantern's glow below accentuates.
He means to teach me all he can, as if
he knows that even time can separate
the edges of the wound that comes from love:
I wonder if he misses them. A shriek
or sudden laugh descends to us from time
to time, reminding us of joy; the leak
of light above us somewhere seems to tame
large moths, who press themselves against the windows.
I know she's getting older; here, in shadows,

I wonder why we celebrate old age.
The silent stars refuse to speculate,
and offer only names that don't assuage
our loneliness. My father, black and white,
is smoking as he speaks mestizo thoughts.
My *tía*'s birthday party carries on;
his accent bothers me. His cigar points,
and Cuba drifts by slowly cross the moon,
a drawn-out, silver cloud. They lived there once.
He tells me we are made every race,
that in our blood the constellations pulse.
The crickets' pleading seems so out of place,
where I, *yoruba,* am never alone
among the many kingdoms in my bones.

The Virgin that my grandmother adored
was hand-carved, trimmed in jewels, and shiny black.
A pair of candles, like respectful guards,
cast light on her from either side. Shellac,
applied to make her more miraculous—
she never seemed to age—formed rivulets
of tears along her cheeks, where someone's brush
once pressed too heavily, as though regret
had entered in the artist's mind. Of sins
the Virgin knew enough, I always thought
on trailing my stooped grandmother, whose hands
would somehow clasp to form a gnarled knot
in prayer—arthritis so afflicted her
that near the end she couldn't even bear

to hold a spoon to feed herself. It was
the pain the Virgin couldn't take away
that made me first mistrust her. She was wise,
but impotent, too patient to be swayed
to intervene against injustice. *Why?*
I'd ask her from the bedroom's gaping door,
afraid to stand beneath the monstrous eye
the mirror set above her was; I'd dare
to taunt her, just as silently, about
the misery of her own people. Dark
and patient, crying frozen tears, without
a sound she answered me: back from the store
my grandmother collapsed, strewn packages
like some shared burden they had borne with grace.

The family across the street is them.
A bumper sticker on their rusty Ford
implores us to ABOLISH RACISM.
My mother frowns at tall weeds in their yard,
the feral cats they feed; "the neighborhood,"
she sighs. Across the street, right there, it's them,
a different culture, spicy smells of foods
that make me hate my not-quite-Cuban home.
At twelve, I like to think that I am white,
as white as The Mahoneys and The Smyths.
My mother cooks us meatloaf, pink creamed beets,
and Tater Tots. I don't play baseball with
their youngest one, because I hear her shout
that I am busy with my homework now;

I open up a book so that her lie
seems less untrue, less something that I know
is wrong, although I'm not convinced of why.
I hear of violence on the radio,
my father muttering "it's just like them."
His disapproval makes him seem more white
to me, just like my teacher Mr. Shem,
a Jew who dyes his hair peroxide-light.
One day, I glimpse the mother, graceful as
she moved—her brownness triggers me to think
this way, as though she were a lioness
that I'd been trained to study—rapid clinks
as pet food filled six shiny bowls. How fast
they rush to her, enshrined at their repast.

When we return from Venezuela, "bronze"
is what my darker skin is called. Six years
of equatorial strong sun (it burns
to tell my pallid cousins of its rays) left fear
that I might be the blackest one of all
my family. I'm glad to be recast
this way, which sounds just vaguely valuable.
In school, the taunts of "nigger" hardly last
at all; December helps to whiten me
until the moniker of "spic" is how
to designate my color. Gradually,
the metal in me proves its hardness; afterglow
of forging what becomes my tarnished soul
illuminates the pages of the tale

I like to tell myself of why I hurt.
There is another race of people, made
of ore extracted from the earth's fierce heart;
at temperatures of thousands centigrade
internally, our blood is molten lava.
My stare can cause an object to ignite,
the tears I cry are scalding, toxic rivers.
I am impervious to others' hate,
and yet ironically I cannot love.
I am descended from the ancient source
of all recrimination, every grief.
My message for the so-called "human race"
is bullets, cannonballs, and bayonets,
each fashioned from the scars we can't forget.

A black man in the ER waits for me.
I take my time, because the sign-out says
he's homeless, alcoholic, probably
a shooter too, complaining of three days
of headache. Fever, not quite 102.
A cough, and short of breath. It's either AIDS
or just another boring case of flu—
a list of other diagnoses fades
as I catch sight of him, half hidden by
the puke-stained, yellow curtain. "He looks fine,"
my intern gripes. A disembodied cry
suggests the possibility of pain—
I notice all the doctors here are white,
while nearly all the patients that we treat

are black, or brown. He stares back, wearily,
as though he knows the next experiment
in which he's made the subject has to be
as flawed as all the others. Once we've spent
a couple minutes on his history—
we'll fill the gaps ourselves—it's time to find
a vein. The Great Society,
Tuskegee, Martin Luther King—though blind,
my stick surprises me with how his blood
so briskly flows, as if by force of habit.
My intern asks me whether we'll exclude
immunocompromise—"I bet he has it,"
she crows—but I am thinking of his eyes,
the blankness of a hope not realized.

Tonight, the New York Liberty take on
their rivals, the Orlando Miracle.
I watch them skeptically at first, but then
I see their power as they shoot the ball,
their graceful, muscled calves and sweaty arms—
the spray of spit made iridescent by
the pop of countless flashbulbs in the Dome,
as Ms. Tamika shouts to Desiree
who scores on her assist. These girls are *huge,*
their heated play a kind of argument
against oppression, ten black women who
seem capable of anything, intent
on winning as they battle near the hoop,
unflappable, frenetic, impossible to stop

as once again they charge down center court.
Before too long, it's like I'm mesmerized,
I'm seeing Amazons and Audre Lorde,
Aretha Franklin, Nefertiti, crazed
old Tituba, the nameless women slaves
escaping North to change their destinies.
The crowd is nothing but its cheering waves
of pure approval, almost on its knees
for more of what these athletes can provide:
not only entertainment's heedless joy
but also the exuberance of pride
in mastery, in the intelligence of play,
in what once seemed the unattainably
humane, great dream, to be this strong and free.

(after Kevin Young)

Today, I'll tell you a little black lie.
Incited by the white-out, angry crowds
were rioting all day; surprisingly,
the *L.A. Times* declared that the white cloud
of dread descending on the city was
enough to terrify suburbanites
behind our neat black picket fences. Ways
to quell the uprising were talked about;
the mayor, in a brilliant move, released
a thousand coal-black crows, symbol of peace,
before assembled legions of police
in uniforms of somber white. I paced
the kitchen while I watched it all in white-
and-black; I killed a roach with just a whit

of White Flag spray insecticide. The day
grew bright and ominous. Catastrophe
was near us, everything was going grey.
A white cat crossed the street in front of me
confirming my suspicion of bad luck;
beyond a neighbor's hedge, white roses grew,
reminding me of putrefaction's look.
Those goddamned filthy vermin, whites and Jews,
were ready to destroy the purity
of all that blackness represented! Soon,
the whole world would be white with enmity,
the sacred darkness of our attic rooms
and basements flooded with an awful dawning
that anyone can plainly see is mourning.

UNDETECTABLE

IV

Phone Messages on Call

I. *Pls call soon. Diarrhea x 2d. PS I have SIDA (AIDS).*

I let the phone ring thirteen times before
she finally picks up. A TV blares

in Spanish in the background, crash of kids
across a dinner table where she's served—

what? Boiled plantains mashed with salt and oil,
or maybe rice and beans again? "I soil

myself in church last days," she says, voice hushed,
in English both too formal and too harsh,

the language she reserves for landlords, case-
workers, and doctors. She's on Fortavase

and Combivir, another one that tastes
"so terrible, like person's garbage waste."

No fever, weight loss, bloody stools—she has
been back to Guatemala, though. She sighs,

as if remembering a better place,
and tells me she felt stronger there, at peace

without the medications, "the *estrés*—
do you eh-speak eh-Spanish?" "No," I say,

pretending I'd not recognize her face,
and then proceed to offer my advice.

II. *She just says she is afraid. Would like to speak with MD.*

"Hello?" The desperation in her voice
is palpable. Past 2 A.M., my house

itself seems hungry for companionship
beyond the usual half-stumbled trip

to bathroom, or refrigerator: things
not done with yesterday start beckoning,

the still unfolded laundry, books in which
I've saved my place whose curling covers touch,

a glass near empty of whatever I
was drinking from it. "Yes," I answer, try

to sound as if I care. "I'm so afraid,"
she says, sole spokesperson for all the night,

which slowly seems to grow more ominous.
I hate the telephone for linking us,

the tiny burning redness of its numbers,
insomniac red eyes, strange demon slumber—

she starts to cry. I want to ask her what
she fears, but I'm distracted by the weight

of what seem shadows in the dark, the creak
of floorboards while her terrified heart breaks.

III. *Lost his Rx for pain pills. Pls page pt ASAP. Pt in pain.*

It's twenty minutes of his history—
the accident that caused his injury

(which by the way was not his fault—both cars
were totaled), bungled surgeries, the scars

they left him with, the rehabilitation
(which he complied with), also meditation,

some chiropractic quack, a bunch of herbs
(did nothing), acupuncture (damaged nerves),

procedures ranging from electric shocks
to needles in the inflamed spinal tracts,

psychiatrists who told him he was fine
(though personality was "borderline,

like that would fucking help")—before he gets
around to asking me for Percocet,

because narcotics are the only thing
that work. It's like an old familiar song,

the pain just like the lover who is lost,
and leaves a soul that begs to be released

but learns that joy is near enough to hell,
that innocence is irreplaceable.

IV. *Pls call back. No further info given.*

The first time that I called a girl picked up.
She had a question—then the line was cut.

Perhaps she worried about pregnancy,
the secret someone wanted it to be

kept safe. Perhaps she wanted medicine,
the pills that helped her mother to stay sane

so that she wouldn't hit her anymore.
Perhaps she wanted something from the store

but was afraid to leave her grandmother
alone because of her bad Alzheimer's

(who didn't mean to when she'd disconnect
the phone). Perhaps she wanted to get talked

back into staying in her father's home,
afraid her dealer boyfriend's business schemes

might be too dangerous. Perhaps she wanted
not anything but to be thought important

for however brief a moment. I guess,
because she never finished her request,

and when I tried to phone her back again,
she didn't answer, though it rang and rang.

V. *ER calling for approval of head trauma.*

An infinite variety of harm:
The shovel to the head, knife gash to arm,

an infant with a burn shaped like an iron
between his shoulder blades. I hear a siren,

that most impersonal of pleas for help,
extinguish in the other sounds of hope

a city offers as I call in my approval: blast
of hip-hop as some teenagers drive past,

the urgent bark of some protective dog,
the rustle of a wind-blown plastic bag

trapezing by my open window. Why
we hurt ourselves defies the MRI

that shows us only where the bullet lodged.
The tinny Beethoven I hear on hold

while Triage locates their M.D. just seems
to heighten the paradox of our genes,

at once engaged in beauty and intent
on its destruction. Where the patient went

in that lost, wailing ambulance is here,
this heart I open, mortal wound of care.

Undetectable

If love is not invisible, then they
should be too obvious to hide. I see
them back to back, in two appointments. One
is doing well, no symptoms of disease
progression; I can tell by his complaints
(of loss of his libido, change in how
things taste) that he intends to live. He cares
about the way he looks, his blonde hair combed
and held by gel in place, his reddish beard
precisely trimmed. I search for something wrong,
but there is little I can recommend;
his physical is unremarkable,
his body perfect as if shielding what
the poet would forgive as humanness,
not even some enlargement in a gland
or some small blemish on his fragrant skin.
I notice their exchange of glances as
they pass each other in my waiting room;
one seems to say he's undetectable,
both hopeful and not consciously unkind,
the other, longing, trying to be brave
despite the numbness in his lower legs
that causes him to limp. Neuropathy,
lymphoma, rectal warts, plus viral loads
consistently above 300K
no matter what new combination I
prescribe; I look at him and don't know what
to say. To touch him seems like overkill,
a gesture that would only make it worse,
its unseen implications like a blow.
He tells me he keeps losing weight, his dreams

as nonexistent as his sleep; behind
his eyes he has sharp pains, his liver
seems swollen now and then, and when he cries
his nose begins to bleed. No physical
exam today; directly to the lab
he goes, his lover looking worried as
he peers up from his paperback. I watch
them both, but it's impossible to see
their love's unmeasurable quantity.

Spiritual, ca. 1999

When I was ill, my organs functioned well
enough. What failed me was something like
my heart, though more internal; filled with gall,
I want to say, because I died of smoke

that I myself did not inhale
that you yourself did not exhale

but that the world disgorged somehow. I died
so slowly it was like I was alive,
the radiation and insecticide
so quiet, watching while we fell in love

a love that no one understands
the love that everyone demands

and so did I. Who knew that in a lover's kiss
there was not just the pleasure of release
but something deadly I could not resist?
My soul was its tormentor and its peace

and in my body, it was done,
and take my body, we are one—

I prayed to television, surfed for God,
but everywhere was culture, everyone
a text. I cried when I was scapegoated;
the virus replicated in my bones

and I will walk one thousand miles
and write pop lyrics for your smiles

except we know that's foolish. Still, I died,
no matter what I did, biology
more powerful than anything I'd write:
song, poem, thesis, or biography,

my words, bereft while I lay dying
these words, so lost among the living.

On Thanksgiving

Fed up with conversation, I excused
myself and went out for a walk. The light
was angling downward over fallow fields
where children played what games I can't recall —

my brothers, cousins, who are married now.
November's chill surrounded me, dry leaves
or solitary birds dark things swept up
by turns in gusts of wind. About half way

through what once seemed an infinite
expanse of corn — the broken, faded stalks
like soldiers whose forgotten fates were sealed
by some invented foe — I found a ball

half-hidden by a clod of earth. It scowled,
its skin all puckered, stitching reddish-grey
in parts undone. The distant houses grieved,
astonished faces of depleted hope;

the night was fast descending. Nothing spoke.
I gave the ugly relic back to dust,
while from the closest chimney rose white smoke
where they were giving thanks, as each one must.

The Same Old Place

A quiet-falling snow makes beautiful
The city's face, like makeup God applies
To hide the imperfections of a world
I thought I understood. The reasons why

A city's face is scarred are known to God,
Who walks beside me, vastly, towards the river.
I thought I understood the reasons you'd
Decided what was best for us, forgiven

That walk we had along the frozen river.
"We'll both be happier," you'd said, and smiled.
Decidedly, it was the best, and it's a given
That neither one of us would play the child

Whose happiness resides in just a smile.
The snowflakes, falling harder, sting my face;
Across a whitened field play a child
And two red dogs. I spot The Same Old Place:

A burst of stinging tears runs down my face.
It's just a pizza place we used to like,
Whose owner's blind old dog "guarded" the place,
A metaphor for kindness overlooked.

"It's just a pizza place I never liked,"
I say, to no one, or to God's cold world,
Its imperfections gone from where I look;
The quiet, fallen snow is beautiful.

Supernumerary Poem with Fruit Pastries that Allegorically Addresses Death

When I was ill with mononucleosis,
Two moon-faced children came to me and said,
"We once were triplets." Feverish, I stared
At their identical pink quadriceps,
Suspicious of the slow pentameter
In which they spoke. A sextant showed the way
To where their sister rest in peace: SEPTEMBER
8th, date of death (not birth), was chiseled on
Her grey nonagonal tombstone. I cried,
For all the decades I had lived in fear;
The twins, who looked to be eleven years
Of age or so, refused the dozen pastries none
Had offered. "Triskaidekaphobia!"
They shrieked. "1492!" was my reply,
Unsure the etymology of *quince*
Was one less than my Spanish sonnet's lines.

On the Virtues of Not Shaving

Some days I don't shave, weekends usually,
and I rejoice as I turn darker, more
overtly masculine, my face the man
I just as easily could have become—
the poet overcoming something like
leukemia to write my masterpiece,
the doctor staying up all night to save
the dying patient who is hemorrhaging,
the homosexual who cruises parks
for sultry, street-lit sex. Some days I don't
shave, whiskers rough and sharp like awful need,
my face the face of terror in the night,
emotions growing over me, a mood
that no one wants to catch me in, a life
I sometimes think I'd like to have destroyed—
the "dirty Mexican" some teacher told
me I was better than, a ne'er-do-well
both purposeless and dangerous, the smoke
from my unfiltered cigarette itself
a scraggly and unruly beard. Some days
I don't shave, mainly out of laziness,
and when I see myself reflected in
a mirror, who I see is not so manly—
just less presentable, but always me,
an ordinary, balding guy who likes
pretending he is someone else, who hates
the harrowed world for its imprisonment,
who doesn't shave some days, if not for joy,
then possibly for something more like sorrow.

The Four Humours

I. Blood

We wondered if the rumors got to her.
I'd seen her with that other girl behind
The Stop and Shop when I was walking home
from school one day. I swear, the two of them
were kissing, plain as that, the grass so high
it brushed their cheeks. I told my teacher so,
and maybe it was her who called their folks.
Before too long, it was like everyone
in town had heard. We waited for them at
the dime store once, where Cedric grabbed her tits
and said *I'll learn you how to love how God*
intended it, you ugly fucking dyke.
Thing was, she wasn't ugly like you'd think.
She had a certain quality, a shyness
maybe, and I'd describe the way she laughed
as kind of gentle. Anyway, we never saw her with
that girl again. They say she got depressed—
shit, at the service all of us got tearful.
I got to thinking what an awful sight
it was, all that red blood—it wasn't in
the papers, but I heard Melissa's mother,
who was the nurse in the Emergency
that night, say how she was just covered up
in blood. I can't think how you bring yourself
to cut your throat like that yourself—I asked
the counselor they called in to the school,
and she said something like, *What better ink*
to write the language of the heart? I guess
it proves that stuff from Bible school they say,
that such a life of sin breeds misery.

II. Phlegm

"My brain is draining from my head,"
he said as once again he blew
his nose. The clock read 3 A.M.;

its second hand swept slowly through
another viscous minute. Dead
to even nurses sticking them

for new IVs, the other ones
slept off their benders soundlessly.
"I'm losing my intelligence,"

he said, and blew. My patience waned.
He thought he was the president:
Dementia, KS, HIV

were printed in his problem list.
"And plus, I'm getting feverish."
I can't recall his name, but I

remember hating him—grim wish
that he would hurry up and die.
Just then, he took my hand, and kissed

the back of it as though I were
a princess in his foreign land.
"My lady, you are beautiful,"

he said, and coughed again. Unsure
of what to say, my own throat burned.
He said, "You can't know what I feel."

III. Bile

A gun went off and killed a little girl
The day my friend was diagnosed with cancer.
I walked through Central Park; a black dog snarled
At squirrels chattering like they had answers.

The day my friend was diagnosed with cancer
I dreamed of killing someone with a knife.
The squirrels, chattering, had likely answers
To all my angry questions about life—

A homeboy threatened someone with a knife
Not far from where a cop showed off his gun,
An angry answer to most questions about life.
I watched the squirrels hop, the yuppies run;

The cop approached the black kids with his gun.
I wondered how much longer she would live;
The squirrels scattered when the homeboy ran.
I wondered if she'd ever been in love,

I wondered who would pray for her to live,
Forgive her for her anger and her weaknesses.
I wondered why it hurt to fall in love.
The cop tried aiming past me, towards the woods.

Forgive us for our anger, for our weaknesses:
Though Central Park, past the black dog's snarls,
The cop gave chase. A skirmish in the woods.
The gun went off—*No!* shrieked a little girl.

IV. Melancholy

We picked at it with sticks at first, until
an older kid named Samuel arrived.
He dropped a heavy rock right on its skull;
we watched as thick black slime began to ooze
from somewhere just below its heart—or where
we thought its heart should be. "Raccoon,"
said someone solemnly. The landscaper—
sweat gleaming, like the polished figurines
my mother wouldn't ever let me touch—
regarded us with keen suspicion from
across the street. We learned what it could teach;
like any body's secrets, the sublime
receded toward the fact of death. I knew
both sadness, and disgust in love's untruths.

QUESTIONS FOR THE WEATHER

The Age-Old Problem of Sentimental Verse

I'll tell you what the problem was.
It started with Italian—words
too musical for sentences

without a heartfelt revelation
or some destructive exclamation,
a language made of many nations

whose sorrows needed to transcend
their conqueror's white monuments,
and then the passionate revenge

of God. The problem didn't stop
with Him; instead, because of hope,
humanity invented tropes

of unrequited love for which
even English was forced to kvetch,
resulting in each lowly wretch

who's dateless on a Friday night
calling himself a poet. Slight
of hand, a cigarette to light—

DiCaprio plays Romeo
(a famous role from long ago)
while blaring on the radio

we hear the very personal
description of a boy whose girl
"means everything" to him. Recall

the problem of what we confess:
perhaps it's terrible, perhaps
we have to learn to love with less . . .

Or maybe just the opposite
is true, because in love, we're yet
forgiven for misusing it.

The Couple

Releasing his determined grip, he lets
her take the spoon; the cube of cherry Jell-O
teeters on it, about to drop as if
no precipice were any steeper, no

oblivion more final. Earlier
today, he hemorrhaged, the blood so fast
a torrent that it splattered onto her.
She washed herself, unwillingly it seemed,

perhaps not wanting to remove what was
his ending life from where it stained her skin.
I watch them now, the way they love across
the gap between them that their bodies make:

how cruel our life-long separation seems.
The ward keeps narrowing itself to that
bright point outside his door—the muffled screams
along a hallway to the absolute—

and as I turn away from them it's not
their privacy, or even my beginning shame
I wish I could escape. It is the light,
the awful light of what we know must come.

After the Weekly Telephone Call

To say I love them seems too obvious,
and not exactly what I think I feel.
We talked as aimlessly as ones who fail
to understand that time's not limitless;

my father asked me to speak up, while Mom
seemed half-distracted by a TV show.
I wanted to explain that years ago
when I professed eternal hate for them

I spoke not knowing that this day would come,
a time when distances would seem adult,
acceptable, with never any doubt
that they'd have their lives, separate from my own;

I wanted to explain that I still need
them, talk to them as if it weren't resolved.
The swept garage, the pancake mix—these selves
of settled dust. Are we what we've denied?—

Like what they gave to me, their thankless son.
Not just religion, not the first car's thrill,
not education, not the terrible
desire to be whole—but love, the love of then,

so unconditional I can't recall
just how it was expressed. A moment in
his suntanned arms at some bright stadium,
the thunderous applause that buoyed the ball

past grandstands he had hoisted me to see;
her patience while I gathered fallen leaves
the shapes of stars, tucked safely in her sleeves,
for some forgotten science project. We

live far away from one another now,
but call each week by telephone, to hear
again what once was so familiar, clear
enough tonight that it almost seemed new.

For a Dear Friend Who Is Grieving

What was it that was lost?
The question haunts me too,
As Boston suffers blasts
Of searing ten-below
Wind chill. Outside, the last

Dry leaves hold fast to branches,
The snow looks pure but isn't.
My friend makes art that dances,
Despite a heart that husbands
What niggardly resources

It chances on: a crust
Of bread she savors still,
A Paris that she trusts
(Kind mistress, who consoles),
A sound, of garbage trucks

Or neighbors bickering,
That soothes as it distracts.
She lost a love, she sings,
A love whose well-honed axe
Divided everything

In somehow less-than-halves.
I yearn to be with her
Tonight; the wind makes heave
The old house I restored
With my own love, whose "leave"

In someplace not so far
(Grand Rounds in Rochester)
Has made me think. What were
Those things I lost? A star
Blinks frigidly out there,

Aligned with all there is
To fear: the endless night,
The utter loneliness,
The lack of words to write.
And yet from silences

My friend's created hope;
She seems so capable
Of persevering, ripe
With wisdom, poised until
The pain abruptly stops

And she recovers that
Lost line—Apollonaire,
Or Auden, plain as fact.
A light goes on next door
And forces from the black

The image of starved trees
Made beautiful by white
(The snow falls fitfully)—
The minutes given weight
As if (he'd say) when we

Part ways they matter more.
From Boston, Paris seems
Both magical and poor,
Whose milder winter scenes
Insist that we endure—

I see that what I lost
Is irreplaceable
As what my friend now has.
She brews her tea; birds call.
I grieve for what that costs.

Love Poem Written Especially for You

Pretend you think I care for you, and this
experiment might work. (Imagine, you
immortalized in verse!) Your tender kiss
is what I will remember most—how new
it seemed to me, how terrible it was
to almost lose you. Then, I will resist
the impulse to divulge your petty flaws,
which came to grow on me. Mourning the past,
next will come how I knew that I was wrong,
betraying you like that, so heartlessly
it's clear that it was me I was hurting.
Pretend you realize by now we'll be
alone tonight, drunk with the end of day.
Can you forgive? Imagine what you'll say.

Living with Illness

One knits, another reads a magazine,
and if they're anything, they're patient as
they wait. What narratives they'll share I can't
imagine; all I know is that they'll need
advice, a new prescription, someone to
sit quietly for just a moment while
they cry. It's not their symptoms, not the noise
of jackhammers enlarging asphalt wounds
outside, it's not their alcoholic wives,
it's not the presidential primary
that's won or lost today—not any of
this hurts, not even when I give a shot
in someone's flabby, freckled arm. What does
it mean, this endless suffering?
(The *U.S. News and World Report,* months old;
the knitting, maybe a misshapen sweater?)
They always come, as if they wanted to
be understood yet not explained, laid bare
as by the temporary freedom of
the flimsy paper gowns I've given them
to lie completely naked underneath—
examining their eyes, I wonder if
they've told me everything, then listen to
their hearts as if I'd never known the truth.

Doberman Pinscher, Dreaming

Her dreams are better than my life,
or so it seems, the way she whimpers
(pitch of delight) a plea, a knife
she uses to relieve the butcher

of that thick steak. Her dreams are better
than my grey life, her trembling
so sensual she must see colors
(red of the blood, its glistening)

no matter what the experts claim.
Her dreams are better than my dull,
depressing life, her sighs a name
for that unimaginable,

transcendent joy of being wild,
the way I wish I lived, so free
I'd understand that dogs do smile,
as Ruby does when in her dream

she finally is off her leash,
legs moving, rib cage heaving, when
she disappears amidst the brush
in forests fierce with life, without end.

Upon Overhearing, "Anyone Can Write Like Elizabeth Bishop"

So that's what they would have us all believe,
These connoisseurs of nothing's spaciousness,
These slightly less-than-mortal, pompous thieves.
I barely could contain my rage at us,

At the collective disregard for art.
How dare they try to calculate the angle
That she first theorized was rain? My heart
Grew fainter as they let their fish hooks dangle,

Expecting they might catch a great white thing
Of equal wisdom if not magnitude.
The worst part was when they began to sing—
How miserly their cords were, rhymes so crude

It seemed like all the world was suffering.
I knew it then, like anyone who's loved alone,
That music isn't anything but wrong
Except when genius begets the tune.

You Can Just See the Cynicism

That everyone in this society just loves
a spectacle is true—and I'll be damned if out
there somewhere some poor fool just can't believe his eyes
when, clicking on his TV set, he witnesses
the mating rituals of warthogs, or some star
who's screaming something barely comprehensible

at news crews come to film his reprehensible
display of wealth as "privately" he weds his love.
Forget the soundless miracle of falling stars;
the former quarterback who finally comes out
is infinitely better fun. Hell, witnesses
who can corroborate the act with their own eyes

(as in, "I saw how he undressed her with his eyes,
that's how I knew that he was unreliable . . .")
—you know the rest, the movie rights, new witnesses
who claim they saw it too, two of whom fall in love
and then divorce before their tell-all book comes out.
Of course, they're disappointed they're not really stars

but what I'm saying is that all of us are stars,
in theory anyway—just look into your eyes
and see the tragedies they must betray, cried out
from still believing nothing is impossible.
Like paratroopers kicking in your heart, your love's
destroyed, but to this crime there are no witnesses.

It's funny over time that what one witnesses
is never as exciting as it seemed — five-star
hotels and fancy restaurants, what's not to love,
right? Villas in the sun, the sheik who puts out eyes
of courtiers he mistrusts, the irresistible
appeal of silken underwear, and don't leave out

the twenty thousand dollars one couple shelled out
to harvest from grad students (there are witnesses)
their ova. What a spectacle! Invisible
now, all the embryos they will create might star
in yet another docu-drama (*Born Three-Eyed*) —
or else, more quietly, they'll live and maybe love

in hopes that no one finds them out, because in love
all things are still forgivable, where even stars
seem patient witnesses with longing in their eyes.

Cuban Canticle in Five Parts

I. "Lucy, I'm Home!"

Believe me when I tell you that I know
the sense of promise in that accent's roar—
the drama of arrival!—how intent
it is on its accomplishments, its spent
yet somehow infinite, simpatico,
American resolve: he's through the door,

his wife is beautiful, his eldest son
is watching satiny gray reruns, all
the day's humiliations gone. I know
it's not that funny when, in the bright glow
of our nuclear-combustible
not quite perfect family, he begins

to talk about his dreams of something better.
I know he wants the best for me, but I
pretend I'm little Ricky and my mother
(she's zany, irresponsible, *alive*)
is telling some kind of terrible lie
that the whole world cannot help but forgive.

II. Bay of Pigs

First of all, Cubans don't know a damn thing
about democracy, and for that matter,
they just don't understand how to be free.
They like white women, and they like to sing.
You can't just send troops down there to be slaughtered.
Can you imagine how much blood there'd be?

We know that the Americans will help.
Their government despises tyranny;
their President is young and very handsome.
They say he likes dark women, and fine rum.
We Cubans understand that to be free
we first must learn how trust gives rise to hope.

III. *Guantanamera*

They say that she was joyous once; they see
her as an emblem of a nation that
was lost, of all that never was regained.
They say that she felt very little pain,
that in the end she faded quietly,
unable to cry out, protecting what

perhaps she saw as one thing she still owned.
When she was humming in the kitchen, I
decided it was music that I'd always keep.
They say that sometimes she would weep,
predicting that the time for her to die
would come before she could return.

I saw her suffer through dialysis
just once. Propped up on cushions, tubes like flames
of red announcing *la santísima*
sagrada virgen curled about her. Shame
commingled with my tears; I leaned to kiss
the girl who danced to *Guantanamera*.

IV. Jews of the Caribbean

My people, of a solitary star,
who wander, searching for a home someplace
among the murderers and thieves, disgrace
is nothing that the world's not known before:
Survival is our new religion here,
and we have nothing else if not our fear.

My people, save the grains of golden sand
from beaches where your footprints were erased,
save postcards, recipes, the ranch laid waste,
save even what your son can't understand:
The loss of something sacred so complete
that even memory defiles it.

V. The Buena Vista Social Club

It's in a movie that I first return.
It isn't all that glamorous, the way
it was back then, when they were young; but still,
there's something magical in how they sway
intoxicated by their music's spell,
their Cuban hearts as prone as mine to yearn

for some lost love. If that old elegance
remains, perhaps it still resides among
the grand old buildings whose lavish decay
would seem a last bequest to weak from strong,
a kind of awful surfeit of romance
for which at last each one of us must pay—

or else, it's still in them, the dignity
with which they gaze into the camera,
their eyes retracing distances so far
it takes a lifetime to arrive to where
I think it may be possible to see
this truth: What a luxury, to be free in art.

On Christmas Eve

One year you gave me lavish jewelry
which I mistook for lasting love.

One year you gave me guileless poetry
which I believed was not enough.

One year you gave me an infection,
and I was glad you were alive.

This year, I give you your reflection.
Look at me, and know my grief.

Next year, we'll give no gifts at all.
You knew I loved you. Night falls.

The Beech Forest

Through deepening green forest—calls of jays
Belying hidden sanctuaries—we
Rode, glinting cycles scissoring the way.
You pulled ahead of me, gradually;

The deepening green forest grew serene.
I didn't fear the insect, jittery
And laquer-black, that slowly seemed to glean
Some truth about me as it crawled my knee;

I knew that it was June who roamed the leaves
Just briefly silvered through deepening green,
The forest not impervious to breeze.
I wanted you to know that I had grown

To love you even more somehow, just when
I wasn't sure; but you were shrinking to
A tiny point I barely could discern
Through deepening, dark deepening green, through

The forest that had offered us its heart
As if to pose a question. By the path,
A sudden clearing opened up: salt marsh,
Or perhaps a swamp? A giant beech beneath

The glaring sun shaded the distant edge.
I pedaled on, though now the forest thinned
To stunted pines less green than gray from age
Until a moonscape made of deep white dunes

Subsumed it all, like hunger. *What it takes,*
I thought. You, waiting for me, patiently;
Out in the distance, ships trailed their long wakes
Like white bridal veils through the deep green sea.

In Case of Emergency Landing

All I could think of was your face as we
descended—light brown eyes, the careful way

you knit your brows. Outside, the thunderstorm
was like a riot of photographers,

the flashes making us seem glamorous.
But I was terrified. A howling gust

demanded sudden movement from the plane,
allowing me to glimpse Chicago's stain

of yellow-orange lights below, a brief
reminder of how little we achieve—

and yet, how very fortunate we are
to populate such cities made of stars,

to live (however fleetingly) if not
in love, then with some kind of safety net

to save us. Call it faith, perhaps; perhaps
it's nothing more than my hand in your lap,

the gentle pressure of your grip that says
we are together, we are here to stay.

Questions for the Weather

*in memory of the victims of the terrorist attacks
of 11 September 2001*

To the wind: remember us. Who's not to say
the airplane roaring overhead in fact
is Armageddon? The wind is cool today,
a kind of calm before the last attack.
The wind is hurling birds across the sky,
enacting distance, pretending what can fly
is always beautiful. Who's not to say
that what we can remember when we die
is really just a single moment? Not a life
of great accomplishments, but a cool wind
that touched us once, less urgently than love,
but as familiar as a long-lost friend.
The wind does not remember us. Yet we'll
remember it, distantly, desperately.

RAFAEL CAMPO is a practicing physician and an assistant professor of medicine at Harvard Medical School. His other volumes of poetry are *Diva* (Duke), which was nominated for the 2000 National Book Critics Circle Award; *What the Body Told* (Duke), which was awarded a 1996 Lambda Literary Award; and *The Other Man was Me: A Voyage to the New World*, which was a National Poetry Series award selection in 1994. He is also the author of a collection of essays, *The Poetry of Healing: A Doctor's Education in Empathy, Identity, and Desire*, which also received a Lambda Literary Award in 1997. He lives in Jamaica Plain, Massachusetts.